AUSTRALIA'S NIGHTINGALE

Nellie Melba

Dedication

To the inspirational women in my life,
of which I am incredibly fortunate to have so many,
to my mother, my nana, my sister, and my friends who inspire me every day,
I dedicate this book to you.

Brolly Books
(an imprint of Borghesi and Adam Publishers Pty Ltd)
Suite 330, 45 Glenferrie Road, Malvern Australia 3145
www.brollybooks.com
email: emma@brollybooks.com

First published in 2016, reprinted 2022.

Text by Cassy Liberman

Illustrations on pages 6, 8, 18, 20, 22, 25, 28, 32, 36, 37, 43, 44 and 45 by Sarah Carter Jenkins.
All decorative border illustrations by Sarah Carter Jenkins.
Illustrations on pages 10-11, 12-13, 14-15, 17, 26-27, 31, 34, and 38-39 by Emma Borghesi.
Composite illustration on page 40 by Sarah Carter Jenkins (Nellie's face and hair)
and Emma Borghesi (other illustrative elements).
Cover and text design by Emma Borghesi.

Printed in India.
ISBN 9781925386042
Cataloguing in publication data is available
through the National Library of Australia

NOTES AND ACKNOWLEDGEMENTS

Painting on page 4: *Portrait of Nellie Melba who sang the role of Ophelia in Ambroise Thomas' opera* Hamlet
(Henri Gervex, 1852-1929 | Lessingimages.com)

Background painting on pages 8-9: *The East India ship* Mellish *entering the harbour of Sydney*
(Edward Duncan, reproduced courtesy of the National Library of Australia).
This painting does not depict the ship that David Mitchell travelled on to Australia but rather is used here
to represent 19th-century sailing ships.

AUSTRALIA'S NIGHTINGALE

Nellie Melba

INSPIRATIONAL AUSTRALIAN WOMEN

by Cassy Liberman

Portrait of Nellie Melba who sang the role of Ophelia in Ambroise Thomas' opera Hamlet
(by Henri Gervex)

Foreword

Everyone wants to be 'happy'.

A primary motivator for everything we do is our desire to be 'happy'. But life is a journey, and that journey is full of ups, downs, bumps, scratches, successes and yes, failures too. Not every moment along the journey can be 'happy'. Our knowledge of what true happiness is requires a certain knowledge of what unhappiness is.

I believe that to be 'happy' requires courage. For courage is about recognising the complexity of the journey of life. Courage is facing our fears, facing our failures and having the determination, fortitude, self-belief and drive to continue to strive towards our goals. It is not merely avoiding situations that create a sense of fear or failure and camping out in the illusions of 'happy'. Courage is what makes the women I write about inspiring. It is what inspires me. It is the ability to walk into the fire and press on, no matter how burnt you get. Because if you can walk through the fire and prove your courage to yourself, you will be as invincible as Nellie Melba. And as happy.

Enjoy the journey,
Cassy

Today Nellie Melba is considered the first international Australian superstar and cultural icon.

She was not born a superstar; no one is. People become superstars through talent, hard work, persistence and determination.

Nellie Melba had all of these. She always knew she would succeed, she never wavered in her determination, commitment and hard work, and she never, ever, wavered in her self-confidence.

Nellie's father, David, travelled from Scotland to Australia by ship in 1852. He was aged just 23 and had only a single gold coin, called a sovereign, in his pocket.

In Melbourne, David met and married Isabella Ann Dow and from humble beginnings he built a thriving, successful business.

In May 1861, their daughter Helen Porter Mitchell was born in the suburb of Richmond. From the time of her birth she was always called 'Nellie'.

Nellie was always full of life, enthusiasm and energy. In fact, she hated to be still! She wanted to be happy and have fun—lots of fun.

She was adventurous: pushing every boundary, challenging every norm. Yet it was more than just a search for fun. With a nursery full of children, Nellie would try anything to get the attention she craved.

But as a result of her pranks and high jinks, Nellie was often considered a naughty and undisciplined child. So she was packed off to boarding school when she was very young in the hope that her teachers could temper her spirit and encourage her to become a young lady of modest and appropriate behaviour.

Relief for Nellie from boarding school and its unending rules came in the form of holidays in the bush, on the outskirts of Melbourne, where her family had 10,000 acres (4046 hectares) of land called Steel's Flats. They would travel there by public coach, pulled along by horses. Nellie, always seeking excitement, sat up top next to the driver.

They were times of freedom and joy for Nellie. Here there was abundant room for her to express her enthusiasm and personality as she swam, fished, ran, rode and sang. Here, she did not need to sit still or be proper. Here, she could just be Nellie.

Nellie lived in an age when women were not equal to men. In fact, women were considered inferior to men. It was even believed that their brains were smaller and less capable. As a result, young girls were not given the same education as boys. The focus of their education was to provide them with the tools to become better wives and mothers, with no thought to a career or a different role in society.

Nellie was very lucky, for her father held no such belief. Nellie learned from her father the value of hard work, discipline and determination. Like her father, she strived for perfection.

When a revolutionary new school, Presbyterian Ladies College, opened in Melbourne, Nellie and her sister were amongst its first students.

At this radical new school, girls were not merely taught how to behave in society, how to keep a home, and how to be accomplished wives and mothers. They were regarded as men's equals and given the same study opportunities.

Here, Nellie found a place where she could express her enthusiasm and her love for life. She was encouraged to pursue her ambitions and to succeed.

From her mother, Nellie gained her love of music. As a young girl, Nellie would sit under the piano while her mother played and the music would seep into her soul. With the encouragement of her mother and her teachers, music quickly became her passion.

At the age of six, Nellie began to perform in the occasional concert. By the age of eight, the newspapers of the day were already describing her as a 'perfect wonder'.

When Nellie was young, however, it was not respectable for women to perform on stage for money. They could perform for charity or for private gatherings, but it was a violation of female modesty for a woman of Nellie's social class to have a career as a singer.

Her father forbade it.

Nellie was determined.

She devoted herself to her music. She began music lessons, singing lessons, organ lessons, practising every day and every free moment. She was so consumed by her music that she often forgot to eat.

She was driven to pursue her own sense of perfection.

And, with each passing year, her ambition to escape convention of all forms and to perform on stage in Europe became more and more focused until she decided it was all she wanted to do.

VERE MITCHE

But then Nellie's mother died. As the eldest of eight children, Nellie became responsible for looking after her siblings, especially the youngest child, Vere, who was still a baby.

Her ambitions faded. She devoted herself to looking after Vere. Unlike Nellie, who was robust from the minute she was born, Vere was a weak and sickly child. She died only a few short months after her mother. The Mitchell family was consumed by loss and grief.

One year later, Nellie was offered the opportunity to travel with her father to Mackay in Northern Queensland where he had invested in a sugar plantation.

It was a journey that took nine days, for at that time there were no planes or cars—unlike today, when we can travel from Melbourne to Mackay in a matter of hours.

Nellie felt a renewed sense of adventure and opportunity, for she had never before travelled beyond Steel's Flats. Suddenly she was freed from the obligations of caring for her siblings and the responsibilities of home life that had been placed upon her. Her world opened to the possibilities of her future.

Once again, Nellie began to dream of performing. Her dreams were further inspired by a small travelling opera troupe that visited Mackay while she was there. Intoxicated with the music surrounding her, she agreed to perform for a number of local fundraising events. With her head in a cloud of music and with attention from a whole society in love with her voice and her infectious spirit, Nellie felt truly alive again.

By the time she returned to Melbourne, she was married to a man she had met in Mackay, Charles Frederick Nesbitt Armstrong. She was pregnant and her ambitions for a glittering career had been rekindled.

Somehow, someday, she knew she would succeed as a famous singer—not just in Australia, but the world over.

Once Nellie set her mind on her goal, nothing would stop her. Not her marriage, not motherhood, not her father's opposition, and certainly not convention. Having already accomplished so much in her short life, she firmly believed she could have everything she set her heart on.

Her husband, however, was a man of the land and city life did not agree with him. When their son, George Nesbitt Armstrong, was born, Charles and Nellie moved back to a small town near Mackay where Charles took a job in the local sugar mill. Unlike Mackay, their local home-town was very small and isolated. There was no social life, no singing concerts, and certainly no fun for a young vibrant woman.

The wet season in the north of Australia brought with it endless rain, humidity and mildew. Everything in their Mackay home began to rot, and with the rot came the snakes and leeches. To make matters worse, the Armstrongs had very little money. Nellie felt very isolated and alone. When her piano, her sole escape from her reality, began to warp from the humidity, she sank into a deep depression.

In the midst of her depression and despite opposition from her father and her husband, Nellie made two choices. Realising she could no longer live with Charles in Mackay, she decided to leave him and return to Melbourne with George where she would dedicate herself to her singing. Once settled in Melbourne, she poured all her energy, determination and enthusiasm into her love of singing and her blossoming career. With her family surrounding her and able to look after George, Nellie spent her time practising, training and performing in charity concerts.

With each performance her confidence grew, as did her audience. The newspapers loved her. Her audience loved her. She was in her element.

Yet once again her life was to be altered dramatically when her father asked her to join him on a trip to Europe. She saw this as a golden opportunity to realise her dream. Frantically she began to save money and to gather 'letters of introduction' to teachers and patrons in Europe. These letters would help her to establish a career in Europe.

Nellie did not intend to return to Mackay and a conventional life with her husband. Nor did she intend to return to Melbourne with her father. With or without Charles, she had decided that she and George would somehow make a life for themselves in Europe where she intended to scale the heights of her dreams. It was therefore vital that she earn as much money as she could performing in Australia, before leaving for a life of uncertainty in Europe. There all she would have to sustain her would be her dreams and her determination.

And so Nellie performed to enthusiastic audiences across Victoria and New South Wales before giving a last concert in Melbourne. The audience were in raptures and the stage was soon covered in flowers from her adoring fans. The newspapers applauded her as the star of Australian music performance. With this encouragement, in May 1886, just before her 25th birthday, Nellie departed on a boat trip that would take two months to reach England.

But the thrill and the excitement of her boat journey was to be a bitter contrast to the persistent rejection she faced upon arrival. Despite all her hard work and dedication, she could not find a teacher to continue her studies, and nor could she find a job.

Nellie was alone in her ambition and very frightened. She also had a young child to look after, and she was running out of options. She wondered whether she would have to return to Melbourne with her father. It was only with her final letter of introduction that Nellie found some small success in London.

But still she was not satisfied. Good was never good enough for Nellie. She was driven to continue her search. She was determined to be the best! So she and George travelled to Paris. It was in Paris that Nellie trained under the famous vocal teacher, Madame Marchesi. In Marchesi, Nellie found a woman who would be both like a mother and a teacher to her, and who would help her to fulfil her dreams. Marchesi instantly recognised that Nellie was a 'star'.

At the Marchesi school, Nellie learned everything required of her to be the best opera singer in the world. Yet the school taught far more than opera singing: it was a finishing school that taught its students how to shine in everything they did, both on the stage and in society. Nellie studied French, Italian, music history, acting and, most importantly, how to talk, eat, and conduct herself in the highest levels of society.

It was at the Marchesi school that Helen Porter Mitchell Armstrong became the prima donna, Nellie Melba. The name 'Nellie Melba' was chosen by Nellie and Madame Marchesi as a stage name that could be easily pronounced and recognised all over Europe.

Nellie wished to honour her home-town of Melbourne of which she was very proud. 'Melba' was the perfect choice.

MME. MARCHESI & MELBA

Nellie, as always, was passionate about learning and succeeding. She would do everything in her power to be the best. Whenever she was faced with a challenge or an obstacle, she never gave up. Instead she saw this as an opportunity to work harder and to be more creative. Defeat was not an option.

In Paris, without the support of her family, Nellie hired nannies to help care for George. But wherever she travelled, George travelled with her.

To be the best in her field required dedication and endless hours of gruelling practice. So Nellie trained and studied and practised, night and day. She trained in the bel canto style of singing, which means 'beautiful singing' in Italian. The beauty of the singer's voice was everything—far more important than her acting. In fact, the bel canto style was so precise that singers were taught not to move their bodies at all while they were singing.

Nellie was taught by Madame Marchesi to 'spin her voice as finely and subtly as a spider draws its silky web from its body'.

The popularity of the bel canto style mirrored the intricate, delicate, floral beauty of the Art Nouveau Age, which extended into art, architecture, decoration, fashion and design. It was an age of beauty, attention to detail and flourishes of excess.

Eventually, Nellie performed in Paris. The enthusiasm of the audience was overwhelming and the applause deafening. Even the critics were astounded. Nellie would sing and her voice was echoed by the flute. Her voice had the trill and lightness of a bird. In fact, she was often compared to a nightingale, the most exquisite songbird in the world.

From Paris, Nellie spread her wings and performed in the great opera houses of Europe. For the next 20 years, she sang every summer at Covent Garden in London. Yet she was more than a leading lady of the opera—she was part of London society and was invited to parties and dinners and balls. Nellie was triumphant.

Every winter, when the opera season ended, Nellie would commence a concert tour. Initially she toured Europe, but as her fame spread she began to tour America as well. Nellie would give as many as 50 performances while on tour. Often her touring company would live in a specially designed train that would take them from city to city. Inside were bedrooms, bathrooms, a sitting room with a piano, a kitchen and rooms for Nellie's many staff.

Wherever Nellie performed, she was a sensation. She was recognised as the greatest singer of the Golden Age of Opera and became a superstar. Soon 'Melba mania' began to follow her wherever she went. Crowds would gather at her hotel, outside the opera, and at the train station. They would cheer, inundate her with flowers, ask her for autographs, and more . . .

On stage, the enthusiasm of the audience was so great that sometimes there were 20, 30, even 40 curtain calls, lasting up to 40 minutes, as the audience demanded to see and applaud Nellie and to shower her with love and praise.

Nellie had become one of the best-known women in the world. She was the celebrity of her time, a time when no women other than royalty had worldwide fame or positions of power and influence. The critics came to view her as the greatest voice of her generation.

Not only did the audience love Nellie, but the composers loved her, too. Several times, composers wrote operas for Nellie. She was the muse that inspired them to write. She was the star that performed the finished operas.

Nellie performed for the Kings and Queens and Princes and Princesses of Europe. She performed private concerts, in the homes of friends and royalty. And she performed in front of thousands of people in grand operas with rich costumes and sets.

Fabulous jewels were part of her image. She would layer ropes and ropes of jewels around her neck so that she was a visual feast of glamour and brilliance for her audience.

In Europe, she would receive presents from admiring fans of diamonds, jewels, pearls, medals, bouquets of flowers—all given with love and adoration.

The greatest recognition she received during her lifetime was when King George V awarded her the Dame Grand Cross of the Order of the British Empire, the highest order of Damehood.

One day, after their divorce was finalised, Charles whisked ten-year-old George away from his boarding school without telling Nellie and took him to live in America.

Once in his father's custody, there was no way for Nellie to find him and nothing she could do to get him back, for in those days a father's rights were greater than a mother's. There were no mobile phones and no internet. Trying to find George without any idea where to look was like trying to find a needle in a haystack.

Nellie never gave up—but for 11 very long, heartbreaking years, George was lost to Nellie.

Nellie never remarried. With George gone to live with Charles, and her family all living in Australia, she based herself in London and devoted herself to her music.

In pursuing her career and her passion for music, she turned her back on a conventional life. She instead embraced the uncertainty and adventure of a life lived constantly in motion, travelling from city to city and from country to country. It was a life that was ultimately more public than private, and a life in which everything was sacrificed to her art.

Although this was the dream she had fought to make her reality, Nellie faced a number of battles. The first was preserving her voice and her health. Often, she would succumb to bronchitis when she was pushing herself to the limits of her physical endurance.

Once, she had to stop singing or even speaking for several months in order to cure a nodule on her vocal chords that threatened to ruin her voice entirely.

Her second battle was with the changing tastes of her audience. As the bel canto style, upon which she had focused her career, fell from favour, Nellie took drama and acting lessons, pushing her voice towards the more modern styles of singing. But despite her efforts and her unquenchable spirit, this was one area in which Nellie had only limited success, for the heavier styles of singing did not suit the timbre of her voice. Underlying all of this was a deep sadness at the separation from her beloved son and her sense of being lonely and homesick.

Nellie would also still get stage fright! In fact, the more famous she became, the more nervous she was, for she knew that her audiences were expecting the best. She could give them nothing less. When it was really terrifying, she would lose her voice. But once on stage, the music would seep into her bones and her voice would flow like a string of pearls.

To ease her loneliness and to fight a hovering depression, Nellie channelled her willpower and determination into working even harder. Whatever her fears, Nellie knew that she must be on the stage. It was her passion, her heartbeat, her life.

At the height of her fame, Nellie stayed at the famously luxurious Savoy Hotel in London.

The Savoy had many marvels that other hotels of the time did not have: electricity, central heating, a 'speaking tube' which allowed each room to order room service (for there were no telephones yet), and each suite had its own bathroom. Even in the best hotels of that time, guests usually had to share one bathroom with other guests.

The Savoy was also revolutionary in that it allowed women to dine and take part in festivities in the dining room. Old customs were gradually changing, and respectable women were being given greater freedoms than before.

Upon being allowed to enter the Savoy's dining room, Nellie was so thrilled with the food that she presented the chef with tickets to the opera. To repay her kindness, the chef created a sumptuous dessert for Nellie when she next entertained guests. The dessert was made with peeled white peaches poached in vanilla syrup, on a bed of ice cream and topped with strawberries. The dessert came on the back of an ice-carved swan—a symbol of the opera the chef had seen. The dessert became so famous that it is still known today as 'Peach Melba'.

Nellie never let the fame overwhelm her. She was full of good will and praise for her fellow performers. She was professional, punctual and exact.

Increasingly over the years she became involved in the 'business' of opera. She formed and often financed the touring companies for which she performed each season.

From an early age, Nellie had been taught by her father the value of money. Once again, David Mitchell was a visionary. Married women had only recently been allowed to attend university, to vote and to own property in Australia and England. Before this time, property was owned either by a girl's father or by a woman's husband. Nellie's financial independence and understanding were both highly unusual and important for her success.

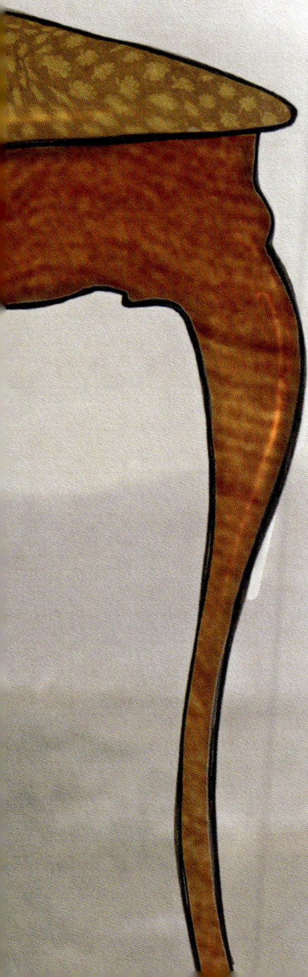

MELBA

Ever the businesswoman and explorer, Nellie was eager to seek out new adventures. It is therefore, no surprise that Nellie was excited by a new invention, the gramophone. For the first time in history it became possible to record a person's voice onto a flat piece of glass and replay it on a gramophone anywhere in the world. Before this revolutionary invention, it had not been possible to capture and record a person's voice, or even a mere sound, and play it back again.

Her first record sold out in a day, despite the high price. Nellie went on to record over 100 records, each of which had many pressings and yet continued to sell out, ultimately selling millions of records. Nellie was also part of the first radio broadcast ever held.

Nellie was excited by the new world of opportunities in the Industrial Age of machines and technology. Opera was no longer just part of the fashionable high society who could afford to go to the theatre. She was now heard in every home that had a radio or a gramophone—in homes that had never before been to or heard an opera.

In 1902, Nellie returned to Australia for the first time since she had left for Europe sixteen years earlier. Then, and with each subsequent return, she was warmly welcomed and triumphant.

In 1904, 11 years after being separated from her son, Nellie was reunited with George. Both mother and son were over-whelmed with joy. From that day forward, Nellie was able to share her life and the rewards of her hard work with her one true love, George. After what seemed like a lifetime spent estranged from her beloved son and country, Nellie finally found herself in their sweet embrace.

A great triumph for Nellie was to sing at the Melbourne Exhibition Building in 1907. This magnificent building, designed by Joseph Reed, was built by her own father, David Mitchell, and is now a World Heritage site. Nellie's father was her hero, even though he had originally disapproved of her career. For Nellie, returning to Melbourne as the most famous opera singer in the world and singing at the Exhibition Building while her father sat with thousands of others in the audience was her proudest moment.

Nellie was the Queen of opera and held a position of immense power and influence. Later, as World War I raged around the globe she used this to raise money for the war effort. She donated generously to charities either by singing without payment at fundraising events or donating money directly. In Australia alone she raised over £90,000 during the war (a staggering amount equivalent to over $2,000,000 today).

She was nicknamed the 'Queen of Pickpockets' because she approached strangers and asked them to promise to give her everything in their purse before they even looked inside to see how much they had. And they did! At her concerts, she would ask the audience to donate generously–and she soon learned to quickly open her umbrella as the coins were thrown to the stage in a shower of generosity.

In Melbourne, Nellie also established a singing school for girls where she would sing and teach and nurture a new generation of Australian opera singers. With the decline in popularity, over time, of the bel canto style of singing, Nellie embarked on a crusade to pass on her skills to her students.

Towards the end of her life, Nellie retired to Coombe Cottage in Coldstream, 27 miles (43.5 kilometres) east of Melbourne, ostensibly to live in peace and quiet . . . but peace and quiet were never her style. Immediately she invited guests to come and stay with her, to fill the house with life and laughter, and to keep the ever-threatening depression, at bay. She was often joined by her son, George, his wife Evie, and Nellie's much beloved granddaughter, Pamela Helen Fullerton Armstrong.

Of course, her several attempts at retirement never lasted long and she would inevitably return to the concert halls of Europe and Australia for a 'farewell' concert performance, time and time again, thus dividing her time almost equally between the country of her heart and the world of adventure and her admiring public.

In February 1931, at the age of 69, Nellie Melba died in Sydney, Australia. To this day, she can be seen on Australia's $100 bill and on two special stamps released by Australia Post. The first was released in 1961, and the second in 2011 to mark the 150th anniversary of her birth.

Nellie will always be remembered as Australia's nightingale: a songbird of purity and exquisite beauty unlike any other.

Terms

letter of introduction

A letter of introduction was considered a necessary and important part of polite society in the 18th and 19th centuries. It was regarded as impolite to talk to a person whom you did not know without a formal introduction. When a personal introduction was not possible, a letter was given instead, by one person, to another, to be used as a means of introduction to a third person, whom the first person knows and the second person (now with the letter in hand) wishes to meet.

Presbyterian Ladies College ('PLC')

PLC was founded in 1875 and is one of the first independent schools for girls in Australia still in existence. Nellie Melba attended PLC from 1875 along with 59 other girls, and left school in 1880. PLC was unique at the time as it sought to offer the same educational classes that were taught at schools for boys and was modelled on the *Public Schools Act 1868* (UK).

Conservatorium of Music

The Conservatorium of Music ceased teaching in 2008 after more than 100 years, and became the Dame Nellie Melba Opera Trust which seeks to nurture young singers of exceptional promise.

David Mitchell

Nellie's father, David Mitchell was an entrepreneur and a businessman. He built many landmark buildings in Melbourne including the Exhibition Building, and Scots Church. For a more detailed description of his ventures you can look at http://oa.anu.edu.au/obituary/mitchell-david-4209

Bel Canto

Bel Canto literally means 'beautiful singing'. It is a style of singing that is smooth and confident, yet also light and joyous. When you hear the Bel Canto style, you can not detect the changes in pitch and tone as the changes are so smooth and subtle that they take you with them rather than shock you into following them.

References

Alliance of Girls Schools Australia, http://www.agsa.org.au/page/Notable_Women/First_Women/Melba_Dame_Nellie_1861-1931/

Blainey, Ann 2009, *I am Melba: a biography*, Black Inc. Books, Melbourne.

Hetherington, John 1995, *Nellie Melba: A biography*, Melbourne University Press, Melbourne

Melba Museum, http://www.nelliemelbamuseum.com.au

Melba Opera Trust, http://www.melbaoperatrust.com.au/about-the-trust/melba-conservatorium/

PLC, http://www.plc.vic.edu.au/our-school_history.aspx

Additional sources

To hear recordings of Nellie Melba, visit my website http://www.inspirationalaustralianwomen.com.au (courtesy National Film and Sound Archive of Australia)

For futher recordings of Nellie Melba, visit the National Film and Sound Archive of Australia's website: https://soundcloud.com/nfsaaustralia/dame-nellie-melba-songs-my

To view footage of Nellie Melba, visit http://aso.gov.au/people/Nellie_Melba/

For further information and teachers notes, visit http://www.inspirationalaustralianwomen.com.au

Thank you . . .

I feel so blessed to have the love and support of my family and friends. To each and every one of you, I give my deepest thanks.

Most especially, I give my thanks to you, Hali. The original manuscript for *Australia's Nightingale* sat on my desk for a year, in the 'too hard', 'not quite right', basket. I couldn't put my finger on the grain of sand that irritated me every time I read it. Hali, always the first person to read one of my manuscripts, you were not even given the privilege for that first year because I knew it wasn't 'good enough'. When I finally gave in and gave you the 'it's really not good' pages, you were able to hand me back the pages, along with the key to their rejuvenation. For your perspective, your sensitivity, your insight, your belief in me and this series on Inspirational Australian Women, I humbly thank you.

My journey would not be possible without the love and affection of my divine children; Gabriel, Jasper and Felix. You brighten every day, and tint every vision in technicolour.

There is nothing so vital as the love and support of a mother. To my ever glamorous, ever inspiring mother, you rock.

To Emma, you are, as always, a visionary, a pleasure to work with and the reason these books see the light of day. Thank you.

To Sara, your style, your expression and the glamour that flows from your 'pen' are inspirational and gorgeous. Thank you.

And the prize goes to . . . Mala and Jasper. For your openness and your enquiring minds.

And finally, to my kindred spirit. Thank you for each and every day of love, laughter, tears, affection, understanding, knowing, searching and grounding. Our life is a truly wonderful adventure.